50 Cooking for One Recipes for Home

By: Kelly Johnson

Table of Contents

- Grilled Chicken Breast with Lemon and Herbs
- Single-Serving Vegetable Stir-Fry
- One-Pan Baked Salmon with Roasted Vegetables
- Microwave Quinoa Bowl with Veggies
- Quick and Easy Avocado Toast
- Pesto Pasta for One
- Tomato Basil Omelette
- Spinach and Feta Stuffed Chicken Breast
- Mediterranean Chickpea Salad
- Single-Serving Caprese Sandwich
- Shrimp and Broccoli Stir-Fry
- Baked Sweet Potato with Black Beans and Salsa
- Easy Margherita Pizza for One
- Single-Serving Chicken Fajitas
- Couscous Salad with Roasted Vegetables
- Quick and Healthy Tuna Salad
- One-Pot Sausage and Vegetable Quinoa
- Single-Serving Beef and Vegetable Stir-Fry
- Microwave Egg Fried Rice
- Classic Tomato Soup for One
- Baked ziti with Spinach and Ricotta
- Single-Serving Teriyaki Salmon
- Spaghetti Aglio e Olio for One
- Stuffed Bell Pepper for One
- Microwave Baked Potato with Sour Cream and Chives
- Easy Chickpea Curry for One
- Single-Serving Chicken Caesar Salad
- Lemon Garlic Butter Shrimp Pasta
- Broccoli and Cheddar Stuffed Chicken Breast
- Quick and Easy Tofu Stir-Fry
- Quinoa and Black Bean Stuffed Peppers
- Spinach and Mushroom Quesadilla
- Baked Tilapia with Lemon and Dill
- Single-Serving Chicken and Vegetable Skewers
- Microwave Risotto with Asparagus

- Pita Bread with Hummus and Mediterranean Salad
- Greek Yogurt Parfait with Berries and Granola
- Single-Serving Eggplant Parmesan
- Cauliflower Fried Rice for One
- Spicy Shrimp Tacos with Lime Crema
- Single-Serving Ratatouille
- Baked Chicken Thigh with Rosemary and Potatoes
- Microwave Mac and Cheese
- Cucumber and Cream Cheese Sandwich
- Single-Serving BBQ Chicken Wrap
- Quinoa and Chickpea Buddha Bowl
- One-Pan Lemon Garlic Butter Chicken Thighs
- Vegetable Frittata for One
- Microwave Baked Beans on Toast
- Caprese Quinoa Salad

Grilled Chicken Breast with Lemon and Herbs

Ingredients:

- 1 boneless, skinless chicken breast
- 1 tablespoon olive oil
- 1 lemon (zested and juiced)
- 1 clove garlic, minced
- 1 teaspoon fresh thyme, chopped (or 1/2 teaspoon dried thyme)
- 1 teaspoon fresh rosemary, chopped (or 1/2 teaspoon dried rosemary)
- Salt and pepper to taste

Instructions:

Preheat the Grill:
- Preheat your grill to medium-high heat.

Prepare the Chicken:
- Pat the chicken breast dry with paper towels.
- Season both sides with salt and pepper.

Make the Marinade:
- In a small bowl, combine olive oil, lemon zest, lemon juice, minced garlic, chopped thyme, and chopped rosemary. Mix well.

Marinate the Chicken:
- Place the chicken breast in a shallow dish or a zip-top bag.
- Pour half of the marinade over the chicken, making sure it's well-coated. Reserve the remaining marinade for later.

Grill the Chicken:
- Grill the chicken breast for 6-8 minutes per side, or until the internal temperature reaches 165°F (74°C) and the chicken is cooked through.
- Baste the chicken with the reserved marinade during the last few minutes of cooking.

Rest and Slice:
- Remove the chicken from the grill and let it rest for a couple of minutes.
- Slice the grilled chicken breast into thin strips.

Serve:
- Arrange the sliced chicken on a plate, drizzle with any remaining marinade, and garnish with additional fresh herbs if desired.

Enjoy:

- Grilled Chicken Breast with Lemon and Herbs is ready to be enjoyed! Serve it with your favorite side dishes or a fresh salad.

Feel free to customize this recipe by adding your favorite herbs or adjusting the level of citrus to suit your taste. It's a versatile and quick dish that's perfect for a satisfying meal for one.

Single-Serving Vegetable Stir-Fry

Ingredients:

- 1 cup mixed vegetables (broccoli florets, bell peppers, snap peas, carrots, etc.), sliced or chopped
- 1 tablespoon soy sauce
- 1 tablespoon vegetable oil
- 1 clove garlic, minced
- 1/2 teaspoon ginger, grated
- 1 green onion, sliced (optional)
- 1/2 teaspoon sesame oil (optional)
- Cooked rice or noodles for serving

Instructions:

Prepare the Vegetables:
- Wash and chop the vegetables into bite-sized pieces.

Heat the Pan:
- Heat the vegetable oil in a wok or a large skillet over medium-high heat.

Sauté Aromatics:
- Add minced garlic and grated ginger to the hot oil. Stir-fry for about 30 seconds until fragrant.

Stir-Fry Vegetables:
- Add the mixed vegetables to the pan. Stir-fry them for 3-5 minutes or until they are tender-crisp.

Add Soy Sauce:
- Pour the soy sauce over the vegetables and toss well to coat. Continue stir-frying for an additional 1-2 minutes.

Optional Additions:
- If using, add sliced green onions and a drizzle of sesame oil for extra flavor. Toss to combine.

Serve:
- Transfer the vegetable stir-fry to a plate.

Serve with Rice or Noodles:
- Serve your single-serving vegetable stir-fry over cooked rice or noodles.

Enjoy:
- Your Single-Serving Vegetable Stir-Fry is ready to be enjoyed! It's a quick, healthy, and flavorful meal for one.

Feel free to customize this stir-fry by adding your favorite protein, such as tofu, chicken, shrimp, or beef. Adjust the sauce to your taste preferences, and have fun experimenting with different vegetable combinations.

One-Pan Baked Salmon with Roasted Vegetables

Ingredients:

- 1 salmon fillet (about 6-8 ounces)
- 1 cup mixed vegetables (such as cherry tomatoes, bell peppers, zucchini, and asparagus), chopped
- 1 tablespoon olive oil
- 1 teaspoon lemon juice
- 1 teaspoon Dijon mustard
- 1 clove garlic, minced
- 1/2 teaspoon dried thyme
- Salt and pepper to taste
- Fresh parsley for garnish (optional)

Instructions:

Preheat the Oven:
- Preheat your oven to 400°F (200°C).

Prepare the Salmon:
- Place the salmon fillet on a baking sheet lined with parchment paper.

Prepare the Vegetables:
- In a bowl, toss the chopped vegetables with olive oil, lemon juice, minced garlic, dried thyme, salt, and pepper.

Arrange on Baking Sheet:
- Spread the seasoned vegetables around the salmon on the baking sheet.

Prepare the Sauce:
- In a small bowl, mix together Dijon mustard and a bit of olive oil. Brush the salmon with this mixture.

Bake:
- Bake in the preheated oven for 15-20 minutes, or until the salmon is cooked through and flakes easily with a fork.

Garnish:
- If desired, garnish with fresh parsley for a burst of color and added flavor.

Serve:
- Carefully transfer the baked salmon and roasted vegetables to a plate.

Enjoy:
- Your One-Pan Baked Salmon with Roasted Vegetables is ready to be enjoyed! Serve it with a side of your choice, such as rice or quinoa.

This recipe is not only easy to prepare but also offers a balanced and healthy meal with the combination of omega-3-rich salmon and a variety of colorful vegetables. Adjust the seasoning and vegetables based on your preferences.

Microwave Quinoa Bowl with Veggies

Ingredients:

- 1/2 cup quinoa, rinsed
- 1 cup water
- 1 cup mixed vegetables (such as bell peppers, cherry tomatoes, spinach, or broccoli), chopped
- 1 tablespoon olive oil
- 1 clove garlic, minced
- Salt and pepper to taste
- Optional toppings: feta cheese, lemon juice, or fresh herbs

Instructions:

Rinse Quinoa:
- Rinse the quinoa under cold water to remove any bitterness.

Combine Quinoa and Water:
- In a microwave-safe bowl, combine the rinsed quinoa and water. Microwave on high for 6-8 minutes, or until the quinoa is cooked and the water is absorbed.

Prepare Vegetables:
- While the quinoa is cooking, chop the mixed vegetables.

Sauté Vegetables:
- In another microwave-safe bowl, mix the chopped vegetables with olive oil, minced garlic, salt, and pepper. Microwave on high for 3-5 minutes, or until the vegetables are tender.

Combine Quinoa and Vegetables:
- Once the quinoa is cooked, fluff it with a fork and combine it with the sautéed vegetables.

Optional Toppings:
- Add optional toppings such as feta cheese, a squeeze of lemon juice, or fresh herbs for extra flavor.

Adjust Seasoning:
- Taste and adjust the seasoning as needed.

Serve:
- Your Microwave Quinoa Bowl with Veggies is ready to be served!

This quick and easy microwave quinoa bowl is versatile, allowing you to customize it with your favorite vegetables and toppings. It's a perfect go-to meal for a healthy and satisfying lunch or dinner.

Quick and Easy Avocado Toast

Ingredients:

- 1 slice of whole-grain bread
- 1 ripe avocado
- Salt and pepper to taste
- Optional toppings: cherry tomatoes, red pepper flakes, poached egg, feta cheese, or a drizzle of olive oil

Instructions:

Toast the Bread:
- Toast the whole-grain bread to your desired level of crispiness.

Prepare the Avocado:
- While the bread is toasting, cut the ripe avocado in half. Remove the pit and scoop the avocado flesh into a bowl.

Mash the Avocado:
- Use a fork to mash the avocado until it reaches your preferred level of smoothness. You can leave it slightly chunky or make it completely smooth.

Season the Avocado:
- Season the mashed avocado with salt and pepper to taste. Mix well.

Spread on Toast:
- Once the bread is toasted, spread the mashed avocado evenly over the surface.

Add Optional Toppings:
- Customize your avocado toast with optional toppings like sliced cherry tomatoes, a sprinkle of red pepper flakes, a poached egg, crumbled feta cheese, or a drizzle of olive oil.

Enjoy:
- Your Quick and Easy Avocado Toast is ready to be enjoyed! It's a satisfying and nutritious meal or snack.

Feel free to get creative with your toppings, adapting the recipe to suit your taste preferences. Avocado toast is not only delicious but also a great way to incorporate healthy fats and nutrients into your diet.

Pesto Pasta for One

Ingredients:

- 1/2 cup pasta of your choice (spaghetti, fettuccine, or your favorite shape)
- 1 cup fresh basil leaves
- 1/4 cup grated Parmesan cheese
- 2 tablespoons pine nuts or walnuts
- 1 clove garlic, peeled
- 1/3 cup extra-virgin olive oil
- Salt and pepper to taste
- Optional: Cherry tomatoes, extra Parmesan for garnish

Instructions:

Cook the Pasta:
- Cook the pasta according to the package instructions in a pot of salted boiling water. Drain and set aside.

Prepare the Pesto:
- In a food processor, combine the fresh basil, grated Parmesan cheese, pine nuts (or walnuts), and peeled garlic.

Blend the Pesto:
- Pulse the ingredients in the food processor while slowly pouring in the olive oil. Continue blending until the pesto reaches a smooth consistency.

Season:
- Season the pesto with salt and pepper to taste. Blend again to incorporate the seasonings.

Combine with Pasta:
- In a bowl, mix the cooked pasta with the freshly prepared pesto until the pasta is well coated.

Optional Garnish:
- Garnish your Pesto Pasta with cherry tomatoes cut in half and an extra sprinkle of Parmesan cheese.

Serve:
- Your Pesto Pasta for One is ready to be served!

This quick and flavorful dish allows you to enjoy the vibrant taste of homemade pesto with your favorite pasta. It's a versatile recipe, so feel free to customize it by adding grilled chicken, roasted vegetables, or any other ingredients you love.

Tomato Basil Omelette

Ingredients:

- 2 large eggs
- 1 medium-sized tomato, diced
- 2-3 fresh basil leaves, chopped
- 1 tablespoon olive oil or butter
- Salt and pepper to taste
- Optional: Grated cheese (cheddar, feta, or mozzarella)

Instructions:

Prepare Ingredients:
- Dice the tomato and chop the fresh basil leaves.

Whisk the Eggs:
- In a bowl, whisk the eggs until well combined. Season with a pinch of salt and pepper.

Heat the Pan:
- Heat the olive oil or butter in a non-stick skillet over medium heat.

Sauté Tomatoes:
- Add the diced tomatoes to the pan and sauté for 1-2 minutes until they are slightly softened.

Add Eggs:
- Pour the whisked eggs into the pan over the sautéed tomatoes.

Sprinkle Basil:
- Sprinkle the chopped basil over the eggs.

Cook the Omelette:
- Allow the eggs to set around the edges. As the edges set, gently lift them with a spatula, letting the uncooked eggs flow to the edges.

Optional Cheese:
- If desired, sprinkle grated cheese over one half of the omelette.

Fold and Serve:
- Once the eggs are mostly set but still slightly runny on top, fold the omelette in half using the spatula.

Finish Cooking:
- Continue cooking for another 1-2 minutes until the eggs are fully set, and the cheese, if added, is melted.

Serve:

- Slide the Tomato Basil Omelette onto a plate.

Enjoy:
- Your Tomato Basil Omelette is ready to be enjoyed! Serve it with whole-grain toast or your favorite breakfast sides.

Feel free to customize your omelette with additional ingredients like sautéed mushrooms, onions, or bell peppers. It's a versatile and quick breakfast option packed with fresh flavors.

Spinach and Feta Stuffed Chicken Breast

Ingredients:

- 1 boneless, skinless chicken breast
- 1 cup fresh spinach leaves, chopped
- 2 tablespoons feta cheese, crumbled
- 1 clove garlic, minced
- 1 tablespoon olive oil
- Salt and pepper to taste
- Toothpicks or kitchen twine

Instructions:

Preheat the Oven:
- Preheat your oven to 375°F (190°C).

Prepare the Chicken Breast:
- Lay the chicken breast flat on a cutting board. Using a sharp knife, make a horizontal cut through the thickest part of the breast, creating a pocket without cutting all the way through.

Season the Chicken:
- Season the inside and outside of the chicken breast with salt and pepper.

Prepare the Filling:
- In a bowl, combine the chopped spinach, crumbled feta cheese, minced garlic, and a drizzle of olive oil. Mix well.

Stuff the Chicken:
- Stuff the spinach and feta mixture into the pocket of the chicken breast, pressing it in evenly.

Secure with Toothpicks or Twine:
- Use toothpicks or kitchen twine to secure the opening of the chicken breast and keep the filling in place.

Sear the Chicken:
- In an oven-safe skillet, heat olive oil over medium-high heat. Sear the stuffed chicken breast for 2-3 minutes on each side until golden brown.

Bake in the Oven:
- Transfer the skillet to the preheated oven and bake for 20-25 minutes or until the chicken is cooked through, with an internal temperature of 165°F (74°C).

Rest and Slice:

- Allow the stuffed chicken breast to rest for a few minutes before removing the toothpicks or twine. Slice the chicken into medallions.

Serve:
- Serve the Spinach and Feta Stuffed Chicken Breast slices on a plate. You can drizzle any pan juices over the top.

Enjoy:
- Your Spinach and Feta Stuffed Chicken Breast is ready to be enjoyed! Serve it with a side of roasted vegetables, quinoa, or a salad.

This dish is not only tasty but also visually appealing, making it a great option for a special solo dinner. Adjust the filling ingredients to your liking and enjoy a delicious stuffed chicken breast.

Mediterranean Chickpea Salad

Ingredients:

- 1 cup canned chickpeas, drained and rinsed
- 1 cup cucumber, diced
- 1 cup cherry tomatoes, halved
- 1/4 cup red onion, finely chopped
- 1/4 cup Kalamata olives, pitted and sliced
- 2 tablespoons feta cheese, crumbled
- 1 tablespoon fresh parsley, chopped
- 1 tablespoon extra-virgin olive oil
- 1 tablespoon red wine vinegar
- Salt and pepper to taste
- Optional: Lemon wedges for serving

Instructions:

Prepare Chickpeas:
- Drain and rinse canned chickpeas.

Combine Ingredients:
- In a bowl, combine chickpeas, diced cucumber, halved cherry tomatoes, finely chopped red onion, sliced Kalamata olives, crumbled feta cheese, and chopped fresh parsley.

Make Dressing:
- In a small bowl, whisk together extra-virgin olive oil and red wine vinegar to make the dressing.

Toss Salad:
- Pour the dressing over the chickpea mixture. Gently toss the salad until all ingredients are well coated.

Season:
- Season the Mediterranean Chickpea Salad with salt and pepper to taste. Adjust the seasoning as needed.

Serve:
- Transfer the salad to a serving plate.

Optional: Lemon Wedges:
- Serve with lemon wedges on the side for an extra burst of freshness.

Enjoy:

- Your Mediterranean Chickpea Salad is ready to be enjoyed! It's a satisfying and flavorful dish that can be served on its own or as a side.

Feel free to customize this salad by adding ingredients like chopped cucumber, bell peppers, or a drizzle of balsamic glaze. It's a versatile and nutritious salad that captures the vibrant flavors of the Mediterranean.

Single-Serving Caprese Sandwich

Ingredients:

- 1 ciabatta roll or a small baguette
- 1 small tomato, thinly sliced
- 2 ounces fresh mozzarella cheese, sliced
- Fresh basil leaves
- 1 tablespoon extra-virgin olive oil
- Balsamic glaze (optional)
- Salt and pepper to taste

Instructions:

Slice the Bread:
- If using a ciabatta roll or baguette, slice it in half lengthwise.

Layer the Tomato and Mozzarella:
- Place the tomato slices and fresh mozzarella slices alternately on one side of the bread.

Add Fresh Basil:
- Tuck fresh basil leaves between the tomato and mozzarella slices.

Drizzle with Olive Oil:
- Drizzle extra-virgin olive oil over the tomato, mozzarella, and basil layers.

Season:
- Season with salt and pepper to taste.

Optional Balsamic Glaze:
- If desired, drizzle a small amount of balsamic glaze over the sandwich for added sweetness and flavor.

Close the Sandwich:
- Place the other half of the ciabatta roll or baguette on top to close the sandwich.

Press and Slice:
- If you prefer a pressed sandwich, you can press it in a panini press or use a skillet and press down with a spatula. Otherwise, you can enjoy it as an open-faced sandwich.

Serve:
- Your Single-Serving Caprese Sandwich is ready to be served!

Enjoy:

- Enjoy this classic and flavorful Caprese sandwich with its combination of fresh tomatoes, creamy mozzarella, and fragrant basil.

This recipe captures the essence of a traditional Caprese salad in sandwich form. It's a perfect option for a quick and tasty solo meal, especially during warmer seasons when fresh tomatoes and basil are in abundance.

Shrimp and Broccoli Stir-Fry

Ingredients:

- 1/2 pound shrimp, peeled and deveined
- 1 cup broccoli florets
- 1 tablespoon vegetable oil
- 2 cloves garlic, minced
- 1 teaspoon ginger, grated
- 2 tablespoons soy sauce
- 1 tablespoon oyster sauce
- 1 teaspoon sesame oil
- 1 teaspoon cornstarch (optional, for thickening)
- Cooked rice for serving

Instructions:

Prepare Shrimp:
- Pat the shrimp dry with a paper towel. If they are large, you can cut them in half for easier bites.

Blanch Broccoli:
- Blanch the broccoli florets in boiling water for 2 minutes or until they are slightly tender but still crisp. Drain and set aside.

Make Stir-Fry Sauce:
- In a small bowl, mix together soy sauce, oyster sauce, sesame oil, and cornstarch (if using). Set aside.

Cook Shrimp:
- Heat vegetable oil in a wok or a large skillet over medium-high heat. Add minced garlic and grated ginger, sauté for about 30 seconds until fragrant.
- Add the shrimp and stir-fry for 2-3 minutes until they turn pink and opaque.

Add Broccoli:
- Add the blanched broccoli to the wok and stir-fry for an additional 2 minutes, allowing the flavors to combine.

Pour in Sauce:
- Pour the prepared stir-fry sauce over the shrimp and broccoli. Toss everything together until the shrimp and broccoli are evenly coated.

Adjust Seasoning:
- Taste the stir-fry and adjust the seasoning if needed. You can add more soy sauce or a pinch of salt and pepper.

Serve:
- Serve the Shrimp and Broccoli Stir-Fry over cooked rice.

Enjoy:
- Your Shrimp and Broccoli Stir-Fry is ready to be enjoyed! It's a quick and flavorful meal for one.

Feel free to customize this recipe by adding other vegetables like bell peppers or snap peas. This versatile stir-fry is perfect for a satisfying solo dinner.

Baked Sweet Potato with Black Beans and Salsa

Ingredients:

- 1 medium-sized sweet potato
- 1/2 cup canned black beans, drained and rinsed
- 1/4 cup salsa (store-bought or homemade)
- 1 tablespoon sour cream or Greek yogurt (optional)
- Fresh cilantro, chopped, for garnish (optional)
- Salt and pepper to taste

Instructions:

Preheat the Oven:
- Preheat your oven to 400°F (200°C).

Prepare the Sweet Potato:
- Wash the sweet potato and pierce it a few times with a fork to allow steam to escape during baking.

Bake the Sweet Potato:
- Place the sweet potato on a baking sheet and bake in the preheated oven for 45-60 minutes, or until the sweet potato is tender and can be easily pierced with a fork.

Prepare Black Beans:
- While the sweet potato is baking, heat the black beans in a small saucepan over medium heat. Season with salt and pepper to taste.

Assemble:
- Once the sweet potato is done, slice it open and fluff the flesh with a fork. Top with warmed black beans.

Add Salsa:
- Spoon salsa over the sweet potato and black beans.

Optional Toppings:
- Add a dollop of sour cream or Greek yogurt if desired.

Garnish:
- Garnish with fresh chopped cilantro for added freshness (optional).

Serve:
- Your Baked Sweet Potato with Black Beans and Salsa is ready to be served!

Enjoy:
- Enjoy this wholesome and satisfying dish as a complete meal.

This recipe provides a balance of carbohydrates, protein, and vegetables, making it a nutritious option for a solo dinner. Adjust the toppings and quantities based on your preferences.

Easy Margherita Pizza for One

Ingredients:

- 1 small pizza dough (store-bought or homemade)
- 1/3 cup pizza sauce
- 1/2 cup fresh mozzarella cheese, sliced
- 1-2 medium-sized tomatoes, sliced
- Fresh basil leaves
- Olive oil
- Salt and pepper to taste

Instructions:

Preheat the Oven:
- Preheat your oven to the temperature specified on the pizza dough package or recipe.

Roll Out the Dough:
- Roll out the pizza dough on a floured surface to your desired thickness.

Prepare the Pizza:
- Place the rolled-out dough on a pizza stone or baking sheet lined with parchment paper.

Add Sauce:
- Spread pizza sauce evenly over the dough, leaving a small border around the edges for the crust.

Add Cheese and Tomatoes:
- Arrange the sliced fresh mozzarella evenly on the sauce. Place tomato slices on top.

Bake in the Oven:
- Bake the pizza in the preheated oven according to the dough instructions or until the crust is golden and the cheese is melted and bubbly.

Finish with Basil:
- Once out of the oven, sprinkle fresh basil leaves over the hot pizza.

Drizzle with Olive Oil:
- Drizzle olive oil over the pizza for added flavor.

Season:
- Season the Margherita pizza with salt and pepper to taste.

Slice and Serve:

- Use a pizza cutter to slice the pizza into manageable slices.

Enjoy:
- Your Easy Margherita Pizza for One is ready to be enjoyed!

Feel free to get creative and add a sprinkle of Parmesan cheese, a drizzle of balsamic glaze, or a dash of red pepper flakes for extra flavor. This simple recipe allows you to enjoy a classic Margherita pizza in the comfort of your own home.

Single-Serving Chicken Fajitas

Ingredients:

- 1 boneless, skinless chicken breast, thinly sliced
- 1/2 bell pepper (any color), thinly sliced
- 1/2 onion, thinly sliced
- 1 tablespoon olive oil
- 1 teaspoon chili powder
- 1/2 teaspoon cumin
- 1/2 teaspoon paprika
- 1/4 teaspoon garlic powder
- Salt and pepper to taste
- 2 small flour tortillas
- Optional toppings: salsa, guacamole, sour cream, shredded cheese, lime wedges

Instructions:

Prepare Chicken and Vegetables:
- Thinly slice the chicken breast, bell pepper, and onion.

Season Chicken:
- In a bowl, mix the sliced chicken with chili powder, cumin, paprika, garlic powder, salt, and pepper. Ensure the chicken is well coated with the seasoning.

Sauté Chicken:
- Heat olive oil in a skillet over medium-high heat. Add the seasoned chicken and cook until it's no longer pink in the center and has a nice sear on the edges.

Add Vegetables:
- Add the sliced bell pepper and onion to the skillet with the chicken. Sauté until the vegetables are tender-crisp and slightly caramelized.

Warm Tortillas:
- In a separate dry skillet or in the oven, warm the flour tortillas.

Assemble Fajitas:
- Spoon the chicken and vegetable mixture onto the warm tortillas.

Add Toppings:
- Customize your fajitas with optional toppings like salsa, guacamole, sour cream, shredded cheese, or a squeeze of lime.

Fold and Serve:
- Fold the tortillas around the filling, creating a fajita, and serve immediately.

Enjoy:
- Your Single-Serving Chicken Fajitas are ready to be enjoyed!

Feel free to adjust the spice levels and toppings according to your preferences. This recipe is versatile and can be easily customized for a delicious and satisfying solo meal.

Couscous Salad with Roasted Vegetables

Ingredients:

- 1/2 cup couscous
- 1 cup mixed vegetables (such as cherry tomatoes, bell peppers, zucchini, and red onion), chopped
- 1 tablespoon olive oil
- Salt and pepper to taste
- 2 tablespoons feta cheese, crumbled
- Fresh herbs (such as parsley or basil), chopped
- Balsamic vinaigrette dressing

Instructions:

Preheat the Oven:
- Preheat your oven to 400°F (200°C).

Roast Vegetables:
- Place the chopped mixed vegetables on a baking sheet. Drizzle with olive oil, season with salt and pepper, and toss to coat. Roast in the preheated oven for about 20-25 minutes or until the vegetables are tender and slightly caramelized.

Cook Couscous:
- While the vegetables are roasting, cook the couscous according to the package instructions. Usually, you can bring 1/2 cup of water to a boil, add the couscous, cover, and let it sit for 5 minutes. Fluff with a fork.

Combine Couscous and Vegetables:
- In a bowl, mix the cooked couscous and roasted vegetables.

Add Feta and Herbs:
- Add crumbled feta cheese and chopped fresh herbs to the couscous and vegetable mixture. Toss gently to combine.

Drizzle with Dressing:
- Drizzle balsamic vinaigrette dressing over the couscous salad. Adjust the amount to your liking.

Season:
- Taste and season with additional salt and pepper if needed.

Serve:
- Your Couscous Salad with Roasted Vegetables is ready to be served!

This salad is versatile, and you can customize it by adding other ingredients like olives, cucumbers, or grilled chicken for extra protein. It makes for a delicious and satisfying solo meal.

Quick and Healthy Tuna Salad

Ingredients:

- 1 can (5 oz) tuna, drained
- 1/2 cup cherry tomatoes, halved
- 1/4 cucumber, diced
- 1/4 red onion, finely chopped
- 1 tablespoon olive oil
- 1 tablespoon lemon juice
- Salt and pepper to taste
- Fresh herbs (such as parsley or dill), chopped
- Optional: Avocado slices, whole-grain crackers, or mixed greens for serving

Instructions:

Prepare Tuna:
- Drain the canned tuna and transfer it to a mixing bowl.

Add Vegetables:
- Add halved cherry tomatoes, diced cucumber, and finely chopped red onion to the bowl with tuna.

Drizzle with Olive Oil and Lemon Juice:
- Drizzle olive oil and lemon juice over the tuna and vegetables.

Season:
- Season with salt and pepper to taste.

Add Fresh Herbs:
- Sprinkle chopped fresh herbs (such as parsley or dill) over the mixture.

Toss Gently:
- Gently toss the ingredients until well combined.

Serve:
- Serve the quick and healthy Tuna Salad on its own, with whole-grain crackers, on a bed of mixed greens, or with slices of avocado.

Enjoy:
- Your quick and healthy Tuna Salad is ready to be enjoyed!

Feel free to customize the salad by adding ingredients like olives, cherry tomatoes, or bell peppers. This simple recipe provides a balance of protein, healthy fats, and vegetables, making it a satisfying and nutritious meal for one.

One-Pot Sausage and Vegetable Quinoa

Ingredients:

- 1/2 cup quinoa, rinsed and drained
- 1 cup chicken or vegetable broth
- 1/2 pound sausage, sliced (choose your favorite variety)
- 1/2 bell pepper, diced
- 1/2 zucchini, diced
- 1/4 cup cherry tomatoes, halved
- 1/4 cup red onion, finely chopped
- 1 clove garlic, minced
- 1 tablespoon olive oil
- 1 teaspoon Italian seasoning (or a mix of dried oregano, basil, and thyme)
- Salt and pepper to taste
- Fresh parsley, chopped, for garnish

Instructions:

Prepare Ingredients:
- Rinse and drain the quinoa. Slice the sausage, dice the bell pepper and zucchini, halve the cherry tomatoes, and finely chop the red onion.

Sauté Sausage:
- Heat olive oil in a large skillet or pot over medium heat. Add the sliced sausage and cook until browned on all sides.

Add Vegetables:
- Add the diced bell pepper, zucchini, cherry tomatoes, red onion, and minced garlic to the skillet. Sauté for 2-3 minutes until the vegetables begin to soften.

Add Quinoa:
- Add the rinsed quinoa to the skillet and stir to combine with the sausage and vegetables.

Pour in Broth:
- Pour in the chicken or vegetable broth. Season with Italian seasoning, salt, and pepper. Stir well.

Simmer:

- Bring the mixture to a boil, then reduce the heat to low. Cover the skillet or pot and let it simmer for 15-20 minutes, or until the quinoa is cooked and has absorbed the liquid.

Fluff and Garnish:
- Once the quinoa is cooked, fluff it with a fork. Taste and adjust the seasoning if needed. Garnish with fresh chopped parsley.

Serve:
- Your One-Pot Sausage and Vegetable Quinoa is ready to be served!

This recipe provides a balanced and hearty meal with the protein from the sausage, fiber from the vegetables, and the nutritious properties of quinoa—all cooked in one pot for easy cleanup. Adjust the ingredients based on your preferences.

Single-Serving Beef and Vegetable Stir-Fry

Ingredients:

- 1/2 pound thinly sliced beef (such as flank steak or sirloin)
- 1 cup mixed vegetables (broccoli florets, bell peppers, snap peas, carrots), sliced
- 2 tablespoons soy sauce
- 1 tablespoon oyster sauce
- 1 teaspoon sesame oil
- 1 tablespoon vegetable oil
- 1 clove garlic, minced
- 1/2 teaspoon fresh ginger, grated
- 1 teaspoon cornstarch (optional, for thickening)
- Cooked rice or noodles for serving

Instructions:

Prepare Ingredients:
- Thinly slice the beef and chop the mixed vegetables into bite-sized pieces.

Make Stir-Fry Sauce:
- In a bowl, mix together soy sauce, oyster sauce, sesame oil, and cornstarch (if using). Set aside.

Heat Vegetable Oil:
- Heat vegetable oil in a wok or a large skillet over high heat.

Sear Beef:
- Add the sliced beef to the hot wok or skillet. Stir-fry for 2-3 minutes until the beef is browned and cooked through. Remove the beef from the wok and set it aside.

Sauté Vegetables:
- In the same wok, add a bit more oil if needed. Add minced garlic and grated ginger, sauté for about 30 seconds until fragrant. Add the mixed vegetables and stir-fry for 3-4 minutes until they are crisp-tender.

Combine with Beef:
- Return the cooked beef to the wok with the vegetables. Mix well.

Add Stir-Fry Sauce:
- Pour the prepared stir-fry sauce over the beef and vegetables. Toss everything together until well coated and heated through.

Adjust Seasoning:

- Taste the stir-fry and adjust the seasoning if needed. You can add more soy sauce or a pinch of salt and pepper.

Serve:
- Serve the Beef and Vegetable Stir-Fry over cooked rice or noodles.

Enjoy:
- Your Single-Serving Beef and Vegetable Stir-Fry is ready to be enjoyed!

Feel free to customize this stir-fry by adding your favorite vegetables or adjusting the level of spiciness. It's a quick and flavorful meal that can be easily tailored to your taste preferences.

Microwave Egg Fried Rice

Ingredients:

- 1 cup cooked rice (day-old rice works best)
- 1/2 cup mixed vegetables (frozen or fresh, such as peas, carrots, corn)
- 1 egg
- 2 tablespoons soy sauce
- 1 tablespoon vegetable oil
- 1 green onion, finely chopped (optional)
- Sesame seeds for garnish (optional)

Instructions:

Prepare Rice:
- If you don't have leftover rice, cook rice according to package instructions and allow it to cool.

Cook Vegetables:
- Place the mixed vegetables in a microwave-safe bowl. Add a splash of water, cover the bowl with a microwave-safe plate, and microwave for 2-3 minutes or until the vegetables are tender. Drain any excess water.

Scramble Egg:
- In another microwave-safe bowl, beat the egg with a fork. Microwave the egg in 30-second intervals, stirring after each interval, until fully cooked.

Combine Rice and Vegetables:
- Add the cooked rice and microwaved vegetables to the bowl with the scrambled egg.

Add Soy Sauce:
- Pour soy sauce over the rice, vegetables, and egg mixture. Stir well to combine.

Microwave to Heat:
- Microwave the combined mixture for 1-2 minutes, stirring halfway through, until everything is heated through.

Drizzle with Oil:
- Drizzle vegetable oil over the fried rice and stir to coat evenly.

Garnish:
- Garnish with chopped green onions and sesame seeds if desired.

Adjust Seasoning:
- Taste and adjust the seasoning, adding more soy sauce if needed.

Serve:
- Your Microwave Egg Fried Rice is ready to be served!

This quick and easy recipe is perfect for a satisfying meal when you're short on time. Feel free to customize it by adding cooked shrimp, chicken, or tofu for extra protein.

Classic Tomato Soup for One

Ingredients:

- 1 tablespoon olive oil
- 1/4 cup finely chopped onion
- 1 clove garlic, minced
- 1 cup canned crushed tomatoes
- 1 cup vegetable or chicken broth
- 1/2 teaspoon sugar
- 1/2 teaspoon dried basil
- Salt and pepper to taste
- 1/4 cup heavy cream (optional)
- Fresh basil or parsley for garnish (optional)
- Croutons for serving (optional)

Instructions:

Sauté Onion and Garlic:
- In a small saucepan, heat the olive oil over medium heat. Add the chopped onion and sauté until it becomes translucent, about 2-3 minutes. Add the minced garlic and cook for an additional 30 seconds.

Add Crushed Tomatoes:
- Pour in the canned crushed tomatoes and stir well.

Add Broth:
- Add the vegetable or chicken broth to the saucepan, stirring to combine.

Season:
- Stir in the sugar, dried basil, salt, and pepper. Adjust the seasoning to taste.

Simmer:
- Bring the soup to a simmer, then reduce the heat to low. Allow it to simmer for about 10-15 minutes, allowing the flavors to meld.

Optional Cream:
- If using heavy cream, stir it into the soup and let it simmer for an additional 2-3 minutes. This step is optional but adds creaminess to the soup.

Adjust Consistency:
- If the soup is too thick, you can add a bit more broth to achieve your desired consistency.

Garnish:
- Garnish the tomato soup with fresh basil or parsley if desired.

Serve:
- Ladle the hot soup into a bowl. You can add croutons for an extra crunch.

Enjoy:
- Your Classic Tomato Soup for One is ready to be enjoyed!

This simple and comforting tomato soup is perfect for a cozy meal. Feel free to adjust the seasonings and add your favorite toppings for a personalized touch.

Baked Ziti with Spinach and Ricotta

Ingredients:

- 1/2 cup ziti or penne pasta, cooked according to package instructions
- 1/2 cup ricotta cheese
- 1 cup fresh spinach, chopped
- 1/2 cup marinara sauce
- 1/2 cup shredded mozzarella cheese
- 1/4 cup grated Parmesan cheese
- 1 clove garlic, minced
- 1 tablespoon olive oil
- Salt and pepper to taste
- Fresh basil or parsley for garnish (optional)

Instructions:

Preheat the Oven:
- Preheat your oven to 375°F (190°C).

Prepare Pasta:
- Cook the ziti or penne pasta according to the package instructions. Drain and set aside.

Sauté Spinach:
- In a pan, heat olive oil over medium heat. Add minced garlic and sauté for 30 seconds. Add chopped spinach and cook until wilted. Season with salt and pepper to taste.

Mix Ricotta Mixture:
- In a bowl, mix ricotta cheese with the cooked spinach. Season with salt and pepper.

Combine with Pasta:
- Combine the cooked pasta with the ricotta and spinach mixture. Mix well to coat the pasta.

Layer in Baking Dish:
- In a small baking dish, layer half of the pasta mixture. Spread half of the marinara sauce over it.

Add Mozzarella:
- Sprinkle half of the shredded mozzarella cheese over the pasta.

Repeat Layers:

- Repeat the layers with the remaining pasta mixture, marinara sauce, and shredded mozzarella.

Top with Parmesan:
- Sprinkle grated Parmesan cheese over the top.

Bake:
- Bake in the preheated oven for about 20-25 minutes or until the cheese is melted and bubbly, and the edges are golden.

Garnish:
- Garnish with fresh basil or parsley if desired.

Serve:
- Your Baked Ziti with Spinach and Ricotta is ready to be served!

This single-serving baked ziti is a comforting and satisfying dish. Feel free to customize it by adding your favorite herbs, spices, or extra vegetables.

Single-Serving Teriyaki Salmon

Ingredients:

- 1 salmon fillet (about 4-6 ounces)
- 2 tablespoons teriyaki sauce
- 1 tablespoon soy sauce
- 1 tablespoon honey
- 1 clove garlic, minced
- 1 teaspoon grated ginger
- 1 tablespoon olive oil
- Sesame seeds and green onions for garnish (optional)
- Cooked rice or steamed vegetables for serving

Instructions:

Preheat the Oven:
- Preheat your oven to 400°F (200°C).

Prepare Teriyaki Marinade:
- In a bowl, whisk together teriyaki sauce, soy sauce, honey, minced garlic, and grated ginger.

Marinate Salmon:
- Place the salmon fillet in a shallow dish or a resealable plastic bag. Pour half of the teriyaki marinade over the salmon, reserving the other half for later. Allow the salmon to marinate for at least 15 minutes.

Cook Salmon:
- Heat olive oil in an oven-safe skillet over medium-high heat. Once hot, add the salmon fillet, skin side down. Sear for 2-3 minutes until the skin is crispy.

Brush with Marinade:
- Brush the top of the salmon with some of the reserved teriyaki marinade.

Transfer to Oven:
- Transfer the skillet to the preheated oven and bake for 10-12 minutes or until the salmon is cooked to your liking.

Baste with Marinade:
- Baste the salmon with additional teriyaki marinade halfway through the baking time.

Garnish:

- Optional: Garnish the cooked salmon with sesame seeds and chopped green onions.

Serve:
- Serve the Teriyaki Salmon over cooked rice or alongside steamed vegetables.

Enjoy:
- Your Single-Serving Teriyaki Salmon is ready to be enjoyed!

This recipe allows you to enjoy the sweet and savory flavors of teriyaki salmon in a convenient single-serving portion. Adjust the cooking time based on the thickness of your salmon fillet for optimal results.

Spaghetti Aglio e Olio for One

Ingredients:

- 1/2 cup spaghetti
- 2 tablespoons olive oil
- 2 cloves garlic, thinly sliced
- 1/4 teaspoon red pepper flakes (adjust to taste)
- Salt, to taste
- Fresh parsley, chopped, for garnish
- Grated Parmesan cheese, for serving

Instructions:

Cook Spaghetti:
- Cook the spaghetti according to the package instructions in a pot of boiling salted water until al dente. Reserve about 1/4 cup of pasta water before draining.

Sauté Garlic and Red Pepper Flakes:
- While the pasta is cooking, heat olive oil in a pan over medium heat. Add thinly sliced garlic and red pepper flakes. Sauté for about 1-2 minutes, or until the garlic is golden and aromatic. Be careful not to burn the garlic.

Combine Pasta and Sauce:
- Add the cooked and drained spaghetti to the pan with the garlic and red pepper flakes. Toss the pasta to coat it evenly with the infused olive oil.

Adjust Seasoning:
- Season the spaghetti aglio e olio with salt to taste. If the pasta seems dry, add a bit of the reserved pasta water to moisten it and create a light sauce.

Garnish:
- Garnish the spaghetti with freshly chopped parsley.

Serve:
- Transfer the spaghetti aglio e olio to a plate and serve with grated Parmesan cheese on top.

Enjoy:
- Your Spaghetti Aglio e Olio for One is ready to be enjoyed!

This quick and flavorful dish is perfect for a satisfying solo meal. Feel free to customize it by adding a squeeze of lemon juice, a sprinkle of black pepper, or extra Parmesan cheese if desired.

Stuffed Bell Pepper for One

Ingredients:

- 1 large bell pepper (any color)
- 1/2 cup cooked ground meat (beef, turkey, or plant-based substitute)
- 1/4 cup cooked rice or quinoa
- 1/4 cup black beans, drained and rinsed
- 1/4 cup diced tomatoes
- 1/4 cup shredded cheese (cheddar, mozzarella, or your choice)
- 1 tablespoon tomato sauce or salsa
- 1/2 teaspoon ground cumin
- 1/2 teaspoon chili powder
- Salt and pepper to taste
- Fresh cilantro or parsley for garnish (optional)

Instructions:

Preheat the Oven:
- Preheat your oven to 375°F (190°C).

Prepare the Bell Pepper:
- Cut the bell pepper in half vertically and remove the seeds and membrane.

Parboil the Pepper:
- Boil a pot of water and blanch the bell pepper halves for about 2-3 minutes to slightly soften them. This step is optional but can help reduce baking time.

Prepare Filling:
- In a bowl, combine the cooked ground meat, cooked rice or quinoa, black beans, diced tomatoes, shredded cheese, tomato sauce or salsa, ground cumin, chili powder, salt, and pepper. Mix well.

Stuff the Bell Pepper:
- Fill each bell pepper half with the prepared stuffing mixture, pressing it down slightly.

Bake:
- Place the stuffed bell pepper halves in a baking dish. Bake in the preheated oven for about 20-25 minutes or until the peppers are tender.

Garnish:
- Optional: Garnish the stuffed bell pepper with fresh cilantro or parsley.

Serve:

- Serve the Stuffed Bell Pepper on a plate and enjoy your flavorful and nutritious meal for one!

Feel free to customize the filling by adding vegetables, different spices, or your favorite toppings. This recipe is versatile and allows for creativity in adjusting flavors to your liking.

Microwave Baked Potato with Sour Cream and Chives

Ingredients:

- 1 medium-sized russet potato
- 1 tablespoon olive oil
- Salt, to taste
- 2 tablespoons sour cream
- Fresh chives, chopped, for garnish

Instructions:

Prepare the Potato:
- Wash the potato thoroughly to remove any dirt. Pierce the potato with a fork in a few places to allow steam to escape during cooking.

Coat with Olive Oil:
- Rub the washed and pierced potato with olive oil, ensuring it's well-coated. Sprinkle salt over the oiled potato.

Microwave:
- Place the prepared potato on a microwave-safe plate and cook in the microwave on high for 5-7 minutes, or until the potato is tender. The exact time may vary depending on your microwave's wattage and the size of the potato.

Check for Doneness:
- To check if the potato is done, insert a fork or knife into the center. If it goes in easily, the potato is cooked.

Slice and Fluff:
- Carefully remove the hot potato from the microwave. Slice it open lengthwise and fluff the insides with a fork.

Add Sour Cream and Chives:
- Spoon the sour cream over the potato, allowing it to melt into the fluffy interior. Sprinkle freshly chopped chives on top.

Season to Taste:
- Add more salt or pepper if desired.

Serve:
- Your Microwave Baked Potato with Sour Cream and Chives is ready to be served!

This quick and convenient method of baking a potato in the microwave provides a soft and fluffy interior. Customize your loaded baked potato with additional toppings like grated cheese, bacon bits, or even a dollop of butter based on your preferences.

Easy Chickpea Curry for One

Ingredients:

- 1/2 cup canned chickpeas, drained and rinsed
- 1/2 cup diced tomatoes (fresh or canned)
- 1/4 cup coconut milk
- 1/4 cup diced onion
- 1 clove garlic, minced
- 1/2 teaspoon curry powder
- 1/4 teaspoon ground cumin
- 1/4 teaspoon ground coriander
- 1/4 teaspoon turmeric powder
- 1/4 teaspoon chili powder (adjust to taste)
- Salt and pepper to taste
- 1 tablespoon vegetable oil
- Fresh cilantro, chopped, for garnish (optional)
- Cooked rice or naan bread for serving

Instructions:

Sauté Onion and Garlic:
- In a pan, heat vegetable oil over medium heat. Add diced onions and minced garlic. Sauté until the onions are soft and translucent.

Add Spices:
- Add curry powder, ground cumin, ground coriander, turmeric powder, and chili powder to the pan. Stir and cook for 1-2 minutes until the spices are fragrant.

Add Tomatoes:
- Add diced tomatoes to the pan. Cook for another 2-3 minutes until the tomatoes soften.

Add Chickpeas:
- Add drained and rinsed chickpeas to the pan. Stir well to coat the chickpeas with the spice mixture.

Pour Coconut Milk:
- Pour in the coconut milk and stir to combine. Simmer for 5-7 minutes, allowing the flavors to meld and the curry to thicken slightly.

Season:

- Season the chickpea curry with salt and pepper to taste. Adjust the spices if needed.

Garnish:
- Optional: Garnish the chickpea curry with fresh chopped cilantro for added flavor.

Serve:
- Serve the Easy Chickpea Curry over cooked rice or with naan bread.

Enjoy:
- Your delicious and easy-to-make Chickpea Curry for One is ready to be enjoyed!

Feel free to customize the recipe by adding vegetables like spinach or bell peppers, or adjusting the spice levels according to your preference.

Single-Serving Chicken Caesar Salad

Ingredients:

For the Chicken:

- 1 boneless, skinless chicken breast
- 1 tablespoon olive oil
- Salt and pepper to taste
- 1/2 teaspoon garlic powder
- 1/2 teaspoon dried oregano

For the Salad:

- 2 cups romaine lettuce, chopped
- 1/4 cup croutons
- 2 tablespoons grated Parmesan cheese

For the Dressing:

- 2 tablespoons mayonnaise
- 1 tablespoon grated Parmesan cheese
- 1 teaspoon Dijon mustard
- 1 teaspoon Worcestershire sauce
- 1 clove garlic, minced
- 1 tablespoon lemon juice
- Salt and pepper to taste

Instructions:

Prepare the Chicken:
- Preheat a skillet over medium-high heat. Season the chicken breast with olive oil, salt, pepper, garlic powder, and dried oregano. Cook the chicken until golden brown on both sides and cooked through (about 6-8 minutes per side). Let it rest for a few minutes before slicing.

Make the Dressing:
- In a small bowl, whisk together mayonnaise, grated Parmesan cheese, Dijon mustard, Worcestershire sauce, minced garlic, lemon juice, salt, and pepper. Adjust the seasoning to your taste.

Assemble the Salad:

- In a large bowl, toss the chopped romaine lettuce with the Caesar dressing until well coated.

Add Croutons and Cheese:

- Sprinkle croutons over the salad and toss. Add grated Parmesan cheese and toss again.

Slice Chicken:

- Slice the cooked chicken breast into thin strips.

Top with Chicken:

- Arrange the sliced chicken on top of the salad.

Serve:

- Serve the Single-Serving Chicken Caesar Salad immediately, optionally garnished with additional Parmesan cheese or croutons.

Enjoy:

- Enjoy your delicious and convenient Chicken Caesar Salad!

Feel free to customize the salad by adding cherry tomatoes, hard-boiled eggs, or avocado if desired. Adjust the dressing ingredients to suit your taste preferences.

Lemon Garlic Butter Shrimp Pasta

Ingredients:

- 1/2 cup pasta of your choice
- 8-10 large shrimp, peeled and deveined
- 2 tablespoons unsalted butter
- 2 cloves garlic, minced
- 1 tablespoon olive oil
- Zest of 1 lemon
- Juice of 1/2 lemon
- Salt and black pepper to taste
- Red pepper flakes (optional, for heat)
- Fresh parsley, chopped, for garnish
- Grated Parmesan cheese (optional, for serving)

Instructions:

Cook the Pasta:
- Cook the pasta according to package instructions in a pot of boiling salted water until al dente. Drain and set aside.

Prepare the Shrimp:
- In a pan, heat olive oil and 1 tablespoon of butter over medium-high heat. Add the shrimp and cook for 2-3 minutes on each side or until they turn pink and opaque. Remove the shrimp from the pan and set aside.

Make the Lemon Garlic Butter Sauce:
- In the same pan, add the remaining butter. Add minced garlic and sauté for 1-2 minutes until fragrant. Be careful not to brown the garlic.

Combine Shrimp and Sauce:
- Return the cooked shrimp to the pan. Add lemon zest, lemon juice, salt, black pepper, and red pepper flakes (if using). Toss everything to combine and coat the shrimp in the flavorful sauce.

Add Cooked Pasta:
- Add the cooked pasta to the pan and toss until it's well-coated with the lemon garlic butter sauce.

Adjust Seasoning:
- Taste and adjust the seasoning, adding more salt, pepper, or lemon juice as needed.

Garnish:
- Garnish with chopped fresh parsley.

Serve:
- Serve the Lemon Garlic Butter Shrimp Pasta in a bowl, optionally topped with grated Parmesan cheese.

Enjoy:
- Enjoy your delightful and easy-to-make Lemon Garlic Butter Shrimp Pasta!

Feel free to customize the recipe by adding cherry tomatoes, spinach, or your favorite herbs for extra flavor. This dish is a perfect balance of citrusy, garlicky, and buttery goodness.

Broccoli and Cheddar Stuffed Chicken Breast

Ingredients:

- 1 boneless, skinless chicken breast
- Salt and black pepper to taste
- 1/2 cup broccoli florets, steamed or blanched
- 1/4 cup shredded cheddar cheese
- 1 tablespoon olive oil
- 1/2 teaspoon garlic powder
- 1/2 teaspoon onion powder
- 1/2 teaspoon dried thyme
- 1/4 teaspoon paprika
- 1 tablespoon breadcrumbs (optional, for a crispy coating)

Instructions:

Preheat the Oven:
- Preheat your oven to 400°F (200°C).

Prepare the Chicken Breast:
- Place the chicken breast on a cutting board. Using a sharp knife, make a horizontal slit along the side of the chicken breast to create a pocket without cutting all the way through.

Season the Chicken:
- Season the chicken inside and out with salt, black pepper, garlic powder, onion powder, dried thyme, and paprika.

Stuff with Broccoli and Cheddar:
- Stuff the chicken breast with steamed or blanched broccoli florets and shredded cheddar cheese. Press the edges to seal the pocket.

Optional: Coat with Breadcrumbs:
- If you want a crispy coating, brush the outside of the chicken breast with olive oil and coat it with breadcrumbs.

Sear the Chicken:
- Heat olive oil in an oven-safe skillet over medium-high heat. Sear the chicken for 2-3 minutes on each side until golden brown.

Transfer to Oven:

- Transfer the skillet to the preheated oven and bake for about 20-25 minutes or until the chicken is cooked through and reaches an internal temperature of 165°F (74°C).

Rest and Slice:
- Allow the chicken to rest for a few minutes before slicing.

Serve:
- Serve the Broccoli and Cheddar Stuffed Chicken Breast on a plate, optionally drizzling with any pan juices.

Enjoy:
- Enjoy your delicious and flavorful stuffed chicken breast!

Feel free to customize the stuffing by adding herbs, sun-dried tomatoes, or mushrooms.

This dish pairs well with a side of steamed vegetables or a simple salad.

Quick and Easy Tofu Stir-Fry

Ingredients:

- 1/2 cup firm tofu, cubed
- 1 cup mixed vegetables (bell peppers, broccoli, carrots, snap peas, etc.), chopped
- 1 tablespoon soy sauce
- 1 tablespoon hoisin sauce
- 1 tablespoon sesame oil
- 1 clove garlic, minced
- 1/2 teaspoon ginger, grated
- 1 tablespoon vegetable oil
- Salt and pepper to taste
- Green onions, chopped, for garnish (optional)
- Sesame seeds for garnish (optional)
- Cooked rice or noodles for serving

Instructions:

Prepare Tofu:
- Press the firm tofu to remove excess water. Cut it into cubes.

Sauté Tofu:
- Heat vegetable oil in a wok or a non-stick skillet over medium-high heat. Add tofu cubes and sauté until they turn golden brown on all sides. Remove tofu from the pan and set aside.

Cook Vegetables:
- In the same pan, add a bit more oil if needed. Sauté minced garlic and grated ginger for about 30 seconds. Add the mixed vegetables and stir-fry until they are tender-crisp.

Combine Tofu and Vegetables:
- Add the sautéed tofu back into the pan with the vegetables.

Add Sauces:
- Pour soy sauce, hoisin sauce, and sesame oil over the tofu and vegetables. Toss everything to coat evenly.

Season:
- Season with salt and pepper to taste. Adjust the sauce quantities according to your preference.

Garnish:

- Optional: Garnish the stir-fry with chopped green onions and sesame seeds.

Serve:
- Serve the Quick and Easy Tofu Stir-Fry over cooked rice or noodles.

Enjoy:
- Enjoy your delicious and nutritious tofu stir-fry!

Feel free to experiment with different vegetables and sauces to suit your taste. This recipe is versatile, and you can add a variety of ingredients such as mushrooms, baby corn, or water chestnuts for added texture and flavor.

Quinoa and Black Bean Stuffed Peppers

Ingredients:

- 1 large bell pepper (any color)
- 1/2 cup cooked quinoa
- 1/4 cup black beans, canned and drained
- 1/4 cup corn kernels (fresh, frozen, or canned)
- 1/4 cup diced tomatoes
- 1/4 cup shredded cheese (cheddar, pepper jack, or your choice)
- 1 tablespoon salsa
- 1/2 teaspoon ground cumin
- 1/2 teaspoon chili powder
- Salt and pepper to taste
- Fresh cilantro, chopped, for garnish (optional)
- Avocado slices for serving (optional)

Instructions:

Preheat the Oven:
- Preheat your oven to 375°F (190°C).

Prepare the Bell Pepper:
- Cut the bell pepper in half vertically. Remove the seeds and membrane, creating a hollow space for stuffing.

Prepare the Filling:
- In a bowl, combine cooked quinoa, black beans, corn, diced tomatoes, shredded cheese, salsa, ground cumin, chili powder, salt, and pepper. Mix well.

Stuff the Peppers:
- Spoon the quinoa and black bean mixture into each bell pepper half, pressing down gently.

Bake:
- Place the stuffed peppers in a baking dish. Bake in the preheated oven for about 20-25 minutes or until the peppers are tender.

Garnish:
- Optional: Garnish the stuffed peppers with chopped fresh cilantro.

Serve:
- Serve the Quinoa and Black Bean Stuffed Peppers on a plate. Optionally, add avocado slices on the side.

Enjoy:
- Enjoy your delicious and nutritious stuffed peppers!

Feel free to customize the recipe by adding ingredients like diced onions, jalapeños, or olives to the filling. These stuffed peppers are a versatile and satisfying meal.

Spinach and Mushroom Quesadilla

Ingredients:

- 1 large flour tortilla
- 1/2 cup fresh spinach, chopped
- 1/4 cup mushrooms, sliced
- 1/4 cup shredded cheese (cheddar, mozzarella, or your choice)
- 1 tablespoon olive oil
- 1/2 teaspoon garlic powder
- Salt and pepper to taste
- Salsa, sour cream, or guacamole for dipping (optional)

Instructions:

Prepare Spinach and Mushrooms:
- In a pan, heat olive oil over medium heat. Add sliced mushrooms and cook until they start to brown. Add chopped spinach and sauté until wilted. Season with garlic powder, salt, and pepper.

Assemble Quesadilla:
- Place the flour tortilla on a flat surface. On one half of the tortilla, spread the sautéed spinach and mushrooms. Sprinkle shredded cheese on top.

Fold and Cook:
- Fold the other half of the tortilla over the filling, creating a half-moon shape. Press it down gently. Place the quesadilla in the pan and cook for 2-3 minutes on each side or until the tortilla is golden and the cheese is melted.

Slice:
- Remove the quesadilla from the pan and let it cool for a moment. Use a sharp knife to slice it into wedges.

Serve:
- Serve the Spinach and Mushroom Quesadilla on a plate. Optionally, serve with salsa, sour cream, or guacamole for dipping.

Enjoy:
- Enjoy your delicious and easy-to-make quesadilla!

Feel free to add other ingredients like diced tomatoes, onions, or your favorite spices to customize the filling. This quesadilla is a versatile and satisfying meal that can be prepared in minutes.

Baked Tilapia with Lemon and Dill

Ingredients:

- 1 tilapia fillet
- 1 tablespoon olive oil
- 1 tablespoon fresh lemon juice
- 1 teaspoon fresh dill, chopped
- 1/2 teaspoon garlic powder
- Salt and black pepper to taste
- Lemon slices for garnish
- Fresh dill sprigs for garnish (optional)

Instructions:

Preheat the Oven:
- Preheat your oven to 375°F (190°C).

Prepare the Tilapia:
- Place the tilapia fillet on a baking sheet lined with parchment paper or aluminum foil.

Season the Tilapia:
- In a small bowl, mix together olive oil, fresh lemon juice, chopped dill, garlic powder, salt, and black pepper. Brush the mixture over the tilapia fillet, ensuring it is evenly coated on both sides.

Bake:
- Bake the tilapia in the preheated oven for about 15-20 minutes or until the fish flakes easily with a fork. The cooking time may vary based on the thickness of the fillet.

Garnish:
- Garnish the baked tilapia with lemon slices and fresh dill sprigs.

Serve:
- Serve the Baked Tilapia with Lemon and Dill on a plate.

Enjoy:
- Enjoy your light and flavorful baked tilapia!

This dish pairs well with steamed vegetables, rice, or a fresh salad. Feel free to adjust the seasonings to your taste preferences. It's a quick and healthy meal that can be prepared with minimal effort.

Single-Serving Chicken and Vegetable Skewers

Ingredients:

- 1 boneless, skinless chicken breast, cut into cubes
- 1/2 cup bell peppers, cut into chunks (use various colors)
- 1/2 cup cherry tomatoes
- 1/4 cup red onion, cut into chunks
- 1 tablespoon olive oil
- 1 tablespoon fresh lemon juice
- 1 teaspoon dried oregano
- 1/2 teaspoon garlic powder
- Salt and black pepper to taste
- Wooden or metal skewers

Instructions:

Prepare Skewers:
- If using wooden skewers, soak them in water for about 30 minutes to prevent them from burning. Thread the chicken cubes, bell peppers, cherry tomatoes, and red onion onto the skewers in an alternating pattern.

Prepare Marinade:
- In a bowl, mix together olive oil, fresh lemon juice, dried oregano, garlic powder, salt, and black pepper.

Marinate Skewers:
- Brush the chicken and vegetable skewers with the marinade, ensuring they are evenly coated.

Preheat Grill or Oven:
- Preheat your grill or oven to medium-high heat.

Grill or Bake:
- Grill the skewers for about 8-10 minutes, turning occasionally, until the chicken is cooked through and the vegetables are charred and tender. Alternatively, you can bake them in the oven at 400°F (200°C) for approximately 15-20 minutes.

Serve:
- Once cooked, transfer the Single-Serving Chicken and Vegetable Skewers to a plate.

Enjoy:

- Enjoy your delicious and flavorful skewers!

This dish is versatile, and you can customize the vegetables and seasoning according to your preferences. Serve the skewers with a side of rice, quinoa, or a fresh salad for a complete and satisfying meal.

Microwave Risotto with Asparagus

Ingredients:

- 1/2 cup Arborio rice
- 1 1/2 cups chicken or vegetable broth
- 1/4 cup dry white wine (optional)
- 1/4 cup grated Parmesan cheese
- 1/2 cup asparagus, trimmed and chopped into bite-sized pieces
- 1 tablespoon olive oil
- 1/4 cup onion, finely chopped
- 1 clove garlic, minced
- Salt and black pepper to taste
- Fresh parsley, chopped, for garnish (optional)

Instructions:

Prepare Asparagus:
- Trim the asparagus and chop it into bite-sized pieces.

Sauté Onion and Asparagus:
- In a microwave-safe bowl, combine olive oil, chopped onion, and asparagus. Microwave for 2-3 minutes until the vegetables are slightly softened.

Add Rice and Garlic:
- Stir in Arborio rice and minced garlic into the bowl with sautéed vegetables.

Pour Broth and Wine:
- Add chicken or vegetable broth and dry white wine (if using) to the bowl. Stir to combine.

Microwave:
- Microwave the bowl, uncovered, for 8-10 minutes, stirring every 2-3 minutes to ensure even cooking. The risotto is done when the rice is tender and has absorbed most of the liquid.

Season and Add Cheese:
- Season the risotto with salt and black pepper to taste. Stir in grated Parmesan cheese, ensuring it's well combined.

Let It Rest:

- Allow the Microwave Risotto with Asparagus to rest for a couple of minutes to let the flavors meld.

Garnish and Serve:
- Optionally, garnish with chopped fresh parsley before serving.

Enjoy:
- Enjoy your quick and easy Microwave Risotto with Asparagus!

This microwave version of risotto is a time-saving alternative to the traditional stovetop method, making it a perfect option for a single-serving meal. Feel free to customize the recipe with additional vegetables or herbs.

Pita Bread with Hummus and Mediterranean Salad

Ingredients:

For Pita Bread:

- 1 whole wheat pita bread

For Hummus:

- 1/2 cup canned chickpeas, drained
- 1 tablespoon tahini
- 1 tablespoon olive oil
- 1 clove garlic, minced
- 1 tablespoon lemon juice
- Salt and black pepper to taste

For Mediterranean Salad:

- 1/2 cucumber, diced
- 1/2 cup cherry tomatoes, halved
- 1/4 cup red onion, finely chopped
- 1/4 cup Kalamata olives, pitted and sliced
- 1/4 cup feta cheese, crumbled
- Fresh parsley, chopped, for garnish
- 1 tablespoon olive oil
- 1 tablespoon balsamic vinegar
- Salt and black pepper to taste

Instructions:

Prepare Pita Bread:
- Warm the whole wheat pita bread in a toaster or microwave until it's pliable.

Make Hummus:
- In a blender or food processor, combine drained chickpeas, tahini, olive oil, minced garlic, lemon juice, salt, and black pepper. Blend until smooth, adding a bit of water if needed to reach your desired consistency.

Prepare Mediterranean Salad:

- In a bowl, combine diced cucumber, halved cherry tomatoes, finely chopped red onion, Kalamata olives, and crumbled feta cheese. Toss with olive oil, balsamic vinegar, salt, and black pepper.

Assemble:
- Spread a generous layer of hummus on the warm pita bread.

Add Mediterranean Salad:
- Top the hummus with a portion of the Mediterranean salad.

Garnish:
- Garnish the Pita Bread with Hummus and Mediterranean Salad with fresh chopped parsley.

Fold and Enjoy:
- Fold the pita bread in half or roll it up, and enjoy your delicious and nutritious Mediterranean-inspired meal!

Feel free to customize the salad with additional ingredients like bell peppers, artichoke hearts, or cherry tomatoes. This meal is not only tasty but also packed with fresh and vibrant flavors.

Greek Yogurt Parfait with Berries and Granola

Ingredients:

- 1/2 cup Greek yogurt (plain or flavored)
- 1/4 cup granola
- 1/2 cup mixed berries (strawberries, blueberries, raspberries)
- 1 tablespoon honey or maple syrup (optional)
- Fresh mint leaves for garnish (optional)

Instructions:

Layer Greek Yogurt:
- In a glass or a bowl, start by layering half of the Greek yogurt at the bottom.

Add Granola:
- Sprinkle half of the granola over the Greek yogurt layer.

Layer Berries:
- Add a layer of mixed berries on top of the granola.

Repeat Layers:
- Repeat the layers with the remaining Greek yogurt, granola, and berries.

Drizzle with Honey or Maple Syrup:
- If desired, drizzle honey or maple syrup over the top for a touch of sweetness.

Garnish:
- Optionally, garnish the Greek Yogurt Parfait with fresh mint leaves.

Serve:
- Serve the parfait immediately and enjoy!

This Greek Yogurt Parfait with Berries and Granola is not only delicious but also provides a good balance of protein, fiber, and vitamins. Feel free to customize it with your favorite fruits or add a dollop of nut butter for extra richness.

Single-Serving Eggplant Parmesan

Ingredients:

- 1 small eggplant, sliced into rounds
- Salt, for sweating the eggplant
- 1/2 cup marinara sauce
- 1/2 cup shredded mozzarella cheese
- 2 tablespoons grated Parmesan cheese
- 1 tablespoon breadcrumbs
- 1 tablespoon olive oil
- Fresh basil or parsley for garnish (optional)

Instructions:

Prepare Eggplant:
- Lay the eggplant slices on a paper towel. Sprinkle each slice with salt and let them sit for about 15-20 minutes. This helps remove excess moisture and bitterness from the eggplant.

Preheat Oven:
- Preheat your oven to 400°F (200°C).

Rinse and Pat Dry:
- Rinse the eggplant slices under cold water and pat them dry with a paper towel.

Coat with Breadcrumbs:
- In a small bowl, mix breadcrumbs with a pinch of salt. Coat each eggplant slice with breadcrumbs on both sides.

Bake Eggplant:
- Place the coated eggplant slices on a baking sheet lined with parchment paper. Bake in the preheated oven for about 15-20 minutes or until they are golden and tender.

Layer Eggplant Parmesan:
- In an oven-safe dish, layer the baked eggplant slices. Top each slice with marinara sauce, shredded mozzarella cheese, and grated Parmesan cheese.

Bake Until Cheese Melts:
- Put the dish back in the oven and bake for an additional 10-12 minutes or until the cheese is melted and bubbly.

Broil for Crispy Top (Optional):
- If you like a crispy top, you can briefly broil the Eggplant Parmesan for 1-2 minutes until the cheese on top is golden brown. Keep a close eye to prevent burning.

Garnish and Serve:
- Garnish with fresh basil or parsley if desired. Serve the Single-Serving Eggplant Parmesan hot.

Enjoy:
- Enjoy your delicious and comforting Eggplant Parmesan!

This single-serving version of Eggplant Parmesan is perfect for a satisfying meal without making a large batch. Adjust the quantities based on your preferences.

Cauliflower Fried Rice for One

Ingredients:

- 1 cup cauliflower rice (store-bought or homemade)
- 1/4 cup carrots, diced
- 1/4 cup peas
- 1/4 cup corn kernels
- 1/4 cup bell peppers, diced
- 2 tablespoons soy sauce
- 1 tablespoon sesame oil
- 1 green onion, finely chopped
- 1 clove garlic, minced
- 1 teaspoon ginger, grated
- 1 egg, beaten (optional)
- Salt and black pepper to taste
- Sesame seeds for garnish (optional)

Instructions:

Prepare Cauliflower Rice:
- If you're using fresh cauliflower, pulse it in a food processor to create cauliflower rice. If using store-bought cauliflower rice, thaw it if frozen.

Sauté Vegetables:
- In a pan or wok, heat sesame oil over medium heat. Add diced carrots, peas, corn, and bell peppers. Sauté for 3-5 minutes until the vegetables are slightly tender.

Add Garlic and Ginger:
- Add minced garlic and grated ginger to the sautéed vegetables. Cook for an additional 1-2 minutes until fragrant.

Add Cauliflower Rice:
- Add cauliflower rice to the pan. Stir well to combine with the vegetables.

Make a Well (Optional):
- Push the cauliflower rice and vegetables to one side of the pan, creating a well. Pour the beaten egg into the well and scramble until cooked.

Combine Everything:
- Mix the scrambled egg with the cauliflower rice and vegetables.

Season with Soy Sauce:

- Pour soy sauce over the cauliflower rice mixture. Stir well to evenly coat everything. Adjust the seasoning with salt and black pepper as needed.

Finish with Green Onions:
- Add chopped green onions and stir to combine.

Garnish and Serve:
- Garnish with sesame seeds if desired. Serve the Cauliflower Fried Rice hot.

Enjoy:
- Enjoy your healthy and delicious Cauliflower Fried Rice for one!

Feel free to customize the recipe by adding your favorite protein, such as diced chicken, shrimp, or tofu. This quick and easy dish is a great low-carb alternative to traditional fried rice.

Spicy Shrimp Tacos with Lime Crema

Ingredients:

For Spicy Shrimp:

- 6-8 medium shrimp, peeled and deveined
- 1 tablespoon olive oil
- 1 teaspoon chili powder
- 1/2 teaspoon cumin
- 1/4 teaspoon cayenne pepper (adjust to taste)
- Salt and black pepper to taste

For Lime Crema:

- 2 tablespoons Greek yogurt or sour cream
- 1 tablespoon mayonnaise
- 1 tablespoon fresh lime juice
- 1 teaspoon lime zest
- Salt to taste

For Tacos:

- 2 small corn or flour tortillas
- Shredded cabbage or lettuce
- Diced tomatoes
- Fresh cilantro, chopped
- Sliced jalapeños (optional)
- Lime wedges for serving

Instructions:

Prepare Lime Crema:
- In a bowl, mix Greek yogurt (or sour cream), mayonnaise, lime juice, lime zest, and salt. Stir until well combined. Set aside.

Season Shrimp:

- In a separate bowl, toss shrimp with olive oil, chili powder, cumin, cayenne pepper, salt, and black pepper until evenly coated.

Cook Shrimp:
- Heat a skillet over medium-high heat. Cook the seasoned shrimp for 2-3 minutes per side or until they are pink and cooked through.

Warm Tortillas:
- Warm the tortillas in a dry skillet or microwave.

Assemble Tacos:
- Spread a spoonful of Lime Crema on each tortilla. Place the cooked shrimp on top.

Add Toppings:
- Add shredded cabbage or lettuce, diced tomatoes, chopped cilantro, and sliced jalapeños if you like it spicy.

Finish and Serve:
- Squeeze lime wedges over the tacos for an extra burst of flavor. Serve the Spicy Shrimp Tacos with Lime Crema immediately.

Enjoy:
- Enjoy your delicious and zesty Spicy Shrimp Tacos!

Feel free to customize the toppings based on your preferences. This recipe is a quick and tasty way to enjoy flavorful shrimp tacos with a tangy lime crema.

Single-Serving Ratatouille

Ingredients:

- 1 small eggplant, sliced
- 1 small zucchini, sliced
- 1 small yellow squash, sliced
- 1 small red bell pepper, sliced
- 1 small yellow bell pepper, sliced
- 1 small onion, thinly sliced
- 2 cloves garlic, minced
- 1 cup diced tomatoes (fresh or canned)
- 2 tablespoons tomato paste
- 1 teaspoon dried thyme
- 1 teaspoon dried oregano
- Salt and black pepper to taste
- 2 tablespoons olive oil
- Fresh basil or parsley for garnish (optional)

Instructions:

Preheat Oven:
- Preheat your oven to 375°F (190°C).

Prepare Vegetables:
- Slice the eggplant, zucchini, yellow squash, red bell pepper, yellow bell pepper, and onion into thin rounds or slices.

Sauté Onion and Garlic:
- In an oven-safe skillet, heat olive oil over medium heat. Sauté the sliced onion until translucent, then add minced garlic and cook for an additional minute.

Add Tomatoes and Paste:
- Add diced tomatoes and tomato paste to the skillet. Stir well to combine.

Layer Vegetables:
- Arrange the sliced vegetables in an alternating pattern on top of the tomato mixture. Season with dried thyme, dried oregano, salt, and black pepper.

Drizzle Olive Oil:
- Drizzle olive oil over the layered vegetables.

Bake:
- Bake the Ratatouille in the preheated oven for 35-40 minutes or until the vegetables are tender.

Garnish:
- If desired, garnish with fresh basil or parsley before serving.

Serve:
- Serve the Single-Serving Ratatouille directly from the oven-safe skillet.

Enjoy:
- Enjoy your delicious and colorful Ratatouille!

This single-serving Ratatouille is a visually appealing dish that showcases the vibrant colors and flavors of fresh vegetables. It's a wonderful way to enjoy a classic French dish in a perfectly portioned serving.

Baked Chicken Thigh with Rosemary and Potatoes

Ingredients:

- 1 bone-in, skin-on chicken thigh
- 1 cup baby potatoes, halved
- 1 tablespoon olive oil
- 1 teaspoon fresh rosemary, chopped
- 1 clove garlic, minced
- Salt and black pepper to taste
- Lemon wedges for serving (optional)

Instructions:

Preheat Oven:
- Preheat your oven to 400°F (200°C).

Prepare Chicken Thigh:
- Pat the chicken thigh dry with a paper towel. Season it with salt, black pepper, and half of the chopped rosemary.

Prepare Potatoes:
- In a bowl, toss the halved baby potatoes with olive oil, minced garlic, remaining chopped rosemary, salt, and black pepper.

Assemble:
- Place the seasoned chicken thigh on a baking sheet or oven-safe dish. Arrange the seasoned baby potatoes around the chicken.

Bake:
- Bake in the preheated oven for about 30-35 minutes or until the chicken is cooked through and the potatoes are tender. The internal temperature of the chicken should reach 165°F (74°C).

Broil (Optional):
- If you like crispy skin, you can broil the chicken for an additional 2-3 minutes at the end.

Serve:
- Remove from the oven and let it rest for a few minutes. Serve the Baked Chicken Thigh with Rosemary and Potatoes hot.

Garnish (Optional):
- Squeeze a wedge of lemon over the chicken for an extra burst of flavor if desired.

Enjoy:

- Enjoy your delicious and aromatic Baked Chicken Thigh with Rosemary and Potatoes!

Feel free to customize the recipe by adding additional herbs or spices to suit your taste. This dish is perfect for a comforting and well-balanced single-serving meal.

Microwave Mac and Cheese

Ingredients:

- 1/2 cup elbow macaroni
- 1/2 cup shredded cheddar cheese
- 1/4 cup milk
- 1 tablespoon unsalted butter
- 1/2 teaspoon mustard (optional)
- Salt and black pepper to taste

Instructions:

Cook Macaroni:
- In a microwave-safe bowl, add the elbow macaroni and enough water to cover the pasta. Microwave on high for 3-4 minutes or until the macaroni is cooked through. Drain the water.

Combine Ingredients:
- To the cooked macaroni, add shredded cheddar cheese, milk, unsalted butter, mustard (if using), salt, and black pepper.

Mix Well:
- Stir the ingredients well to combine. Make sure the cheese, butter, and milk evenly coat the macaroni.

Microwave:
- Microwave the mixture on high for 1-2 minutes. Pause and stir every 30 seconds to ensure the cheese melts and forms a creamy sauce.

Check Consistency:
- Adjust the consistency by adding more milk if needed. Continue microwaving in short intervals if necessary.

Serve:
- Once the cheese is fully melted, and the sauce is creamy, your Microwave Mac and Cheese is ready to be served.

Enjoy:
- Enjoy your quick and easy Microwave Mac and Cheese immediately!

This recipe is perfect for a single serving and can be customized with additional ingredients like cooked bacon, sautéed onions, or a pinch of cayenne pepper for added flavor.

Cucumber and Cream Cheese Sandwich

Ingredients:

- 2 slices of your favorite bread
- 2-3 tablespoons cream cheese, softened
- 1/2 cucumber, thinly sliced
- Salt and black pepper to taste
- Fresh dill or chives for garnish (optional)

Instructions:

Prepare Bread:
- Lay out two slices of your chosen bread on a clean surface.

Spread Cream Cheese:
- Spread a generous layer of softened cream cheese on one or both slices of bread.

Add Cucumber Slices:
- Arrange the thinly sliced cucumber evenly over the cream cheese layer.

Season:
- Sprinkle a pinch of salt and black pepper over the cucumber slices. This enhances the flavors.

Garnish (Optional):
- Optionally, garnish with fresh dill or chives for added freshness and flavor.

Assemble:
- Place the second slice of bread on top, creating a sandwich.

Cut and Serve:
- If desired, cut the sandwich into halves or quarters. Serve immediately.

Enjoy:
- Enjoy your light and delightful Cucumber and Cream Cheese Sandwich!

This sandwich is perfect for a quick and refreshing lunch or snack. Feel free to customize it by adding other ingredients like lettuce, sprouts, or avocado if you like.

Single-Serving BBQ Chicken Wrap

Ingredients:

- 1 small chicken breast, cooked and shredded
- 1 tablespoon barbecue sauce
- 1 large whole wheat or spinach tortilla
- 1/4 cup shredded cheddar cheese
- 1/4 cup shredded lettuce
- 1/4 cup diced tomatoes
- 2 tablespoons diced red onion
- 1 tablespoon chopped fresh cilantro or parsley (optional)
- Ranch or Greek yogurt dressing for drizzling (optional)

Instructions:

Prepare Shredded Chicken:
- Cook a small chicken breast (grilled, baked, or pan-seared) until fully cooked. Shred the chicken using two forks.

Mix with BBQ Sauce:
- In a bowl, mix the shredded chicken with barbecue sauce until well coated.

Warm Tortilla:
- Warm the whole wheat or spinach tortilla in a dry skillet or microwave for a few seconds until pliable.

Assemble the Wrap:
- Place the warmed tortilla on a flat surface. Spread the barbecue chicken mixture in the center of the tortilla.

Add Toppings:
- Sprinkle shredded cheddar cheese over the chicken, followed by shredded lettuce, diced tomatoes, diced red onion, and chopped cilantro or parsley if using.

Drizzle Dressing (Optional):
- Optionally, drizzle ranch or Greek yogurt dressing over the toppings for extra flavor.

Fold and Roll:
- Fold the sides of the tortilla in and then roll it up from the bottom, creating a wrap.

Cut and Serve:

- If desired, cut the BBQ Chicken Wrap in half at a diagonal. Secure with toothpicks if needed.

Enjoy:
- Enjoy your tasty and convenient Single-Serving BBQ Chicken Wrap!

Feel free to customize the wrap with additional ingredients such as avocado, bacon, or your favorite veggies. This recipe is versatile and can be adapted to suit your preferences.

Quinoa and Chickpea Buddha Bowl

Ingredients:

For Quinoa:

- 1/2 cup quinoa, rinsed
- 1 cup water
- Pinch of salt

For Chickpeas:

- 1/2 cup canned chickpeas, drained and rinsed
- 1 tablespoon olive oil
- 1/2 teaspoon ground cumin
- 1/2 teaspoon smoked paprika
- Salt and black pepper to taste

For Buddha Bowl:

- 1 cup mixed greens (spinach, kale, arugula, etc.)
- 1/2 cucumber, sliced
- 1/2 avocado, sliced
- 1/4 cup cherry tomatoes, halved
- 1/4 cup shredded carrots
- 2 tablespoons hummus
- Lemon wedges for serving
- Fresh herbs (cilantro, parsley) for garnish (optional)

Instructions:

Cook Quinoa:
- In a saucepan, combine rinsed quinoa, water, and a pinch of salt. Bring to a boil, then reduce heat, cover, and simmer for 15-20 minutes or until the quinoa is cooked and water is absorbed. Fluff with a fork.

Roast Chickpeas:

- Preheat the oven to 400°F (200°C). In a bowl, toss chickpeas with olive oil, ground cumin, smoked paprika, salt, and black pepper. Spread them on a baking sheet and roast in the oven for 20-25 minutes or until crispy.

Assemble Buddha Bowl:
- In a bowl, arrange cooked quinoa, roasted chickpeas, mixed greens, sliced cucumber, avocado, cherry tomatoes, and shredded carrots.

Add Hummus:
- Dollop hummus in the center of the bowl or distribute it over the ingredients.

Garnish:
- Garnish with fresh herbs if desired and squeeze lemon wedges over the bowl for added freshness.

Enjoy:
- Enjoy your vibrant and nutrient-packed Quinoa and Chickpea Buddha Bowl!

Feel free to customize the Buddha Bowl with additional toppings like roasted sweet potatoes, bell peppers, or a drizzle of your favorite dressing. This bowl provides a well-balanced combination of protein, fiber, and healthy fats.

One-Pan Lemon Garlic Butter Chicken Thighs

Ingredients:

- 4 bone-in, skin-on chicken thighs
- Salt and black pepper to taste
- 1 teaspoon paprika
- 1 teaspoon dried thyme
- 2 tablespoons olive oil
- 4 cloves garlic, minced
- Juice of 1 lemon
- 1/2 cup chicken broth
- 2 tablespoons unsalted butter
- Fresh parsley for garnish (optional)

Instructions:

Preheat Oven:
- Preheat your oven to 400°F (200°C).

Season Chicken Thighs:
- Pat the chicken thighs dry with a paper towel. Season both sides with salt, black pepper, paprika, and dried thyme.

Sear Chicken Thighs:
- In an oven-safe skillet, heat olive oil over medium-high heat. Place the seasoned chicken thighs skin-side down and sear for 3-4 minutes until golden brown. Flip and sear for an additional 2 minutes.

Add Garlic:
- Add minced garlic to the skillet and sauté for about 1 minute until fragrant.

Deglaze with Lemon Juice:
- Pour the lemon juice over the chicken, deglazing the pan by scraping up any browned bits from the bottom.

Add Chicken Broth:
- Pour in the chicken broth around the chicken thighs.

Bake:
- Transfer the skillet to the preheated oven and bake for 25-30 minutes or until the chicken is cooked through, and the skin is crispy.

Finish with Butter:
- In the last 5 minutes of baking, add small pieces of unsalted butter over each chicken thigh for a rich and flavorful finish.

Garnish:
- Optionally, garnish with fresh parsley for added freshness.

Serve:
- Serve the One-Pan Lemon Garlic Butter Chicken Thighs hot from the oven.

Enjoy:
- Enjoy your juicy and flavorful one-pan chicken dish!

This recipe is not only delicious but also convenient as it uses just one pan, making cleanup a breeze. Feel free to pair it with your favorite side dishes or a simple salad for a complete meal.

Vegetable Frittata for One

Ingredients:

- 2 large eggs
- 2 tablespoons milk
- Salt and black pepper to taste
- 1 tablespoon olive oil
- 1/4 cup diced bell peppers (any color)
- 1/4 cup diced tomatoes
- 1/4 cup chopped spinach or kale
- 2 tablespoons diced red onion
- 2 tablespoons shredded cheese (cheddar, feta, or your choice)
- Fresh herbs (parsley, chives) for garnish (optional)

Instructions:

Preheat Oven:
- Preheat your oven's broiler.

Whisk Eggs:
- In a bowl, whisk together eggs, milk, salt, and black pepper until well combined.

Prepare Vegetables:
- In an oven-safe skillet, heat olive oil over medium heat. Add diced bell peppers, tomatoes, chopped spinach or kale, and diced red onion. Cook for 2-3 minutes until vegetables are slightly softened.

Add Eggs:
- Pour the whisked eggs over the sautéed vegetables in the skillet.

Cook on Stovetop:
- Allow the frittata to cook on the stovetop for 2-3 minutes without stirring. This helps the edges set.

Add Cheese:
- Sprinkle shredded cheese evenly over the frittata.

Broil in Oven:
- Transfer the skillet to the preheated broiler and cook for an additional 2-3 minutes or until the top is set and slightly golden.

Garnish:
- Optionally, garnish with fresh herbs for added flavor.

Serve:

- Serve the Vegetable Frittata directly from the skillet.

Enjoy:
- Enjoy your delicious and customizable Vegetable Frittata for one!

Feel free to customize the frittata with your favorite vegetables, herbs, or cheese. It's a versatile dish that can be enjoyed for breakfast, brunch, or a quick and satisfying dinner.

Microwave Baked Beans on Toast

Ingredients:

- 1 can (about 15 ounces) baked beans in tomato sauce
- 2 slices of your favorite bread (white, whole wheat, or multigrain)
- Butter for spreading (optional)
- Salt and black pepper to taste
- Optional toppings: grated cheese, chopped parsley, hot sauce, or a fried egg

Instructions:

Prepare Toast:
- Toast the slices of bread to your liking. You can use a toaster, toaster oven, or even a regular oven.

Heat Baked Beans:
- While the bread is toasting, empty the can of baked beans into a microwave-safe bowl. Heat the beans in the microwave according to the package instructions.

Butter Toast (Optional):
- If desired, spread butter on the toasted bread for added richness.

Assembly:
- Pour the heated baked beans over the toasted bread slices.

Season:
- Season the beans with salt and black pepper to taste. Stir gently to combine.

Add Toppings (Optional):
- Customize your Microwave Baked Beans on Toast by adding toppings like grated cheese, chopped parsley, hot sauce, or a fried egg.

Serve:
- Serve the Microwave Baked Beans on Toast immediately while warm.

Enjoy:
- Enjoy your quick and comforting meal!

This Microwave Baked Beans on Toast is a classic and satisfying dish that can be prepared in just a few minutes. It's perfect for a quick breakfast, lunch, or dinner.

Caprese Quinoa Salad

Ingredients:

- 1 cup cooked quinoa, cooled
- 1 cup cherry tomatoes, halved
- 1 cup fresh mozzarella balls, or diced mozzarella
- 1/4 cup fresh basil leaves, torn
- 2 tablespoons extra-virgin olive oil
- 1 tablespoon balsamic glaze or balsamic vinegar
- Salt and black pepper to taste

Instructions:

Cook Quinoa:
- Cook 1/2 cup of quinoa according to package instructions. Once cooked, let it cool.

Prepare Vegetables:
- In a large bowl, combine the cooled quinoa, cherry tomatoes (halved), fresh mozzarella balls, and torn basil leaves.

Make Dressing:
- In a small bowl, whisk together extra-virgin olive oil and balsamic glaze. Season with salt and black pepper to taste.

Combine Ingredients:
- Drizzle the dressing over the quinoa mixture. Gently toss until all ingredients are well combined.

Chill (Optional):
- If time allows, refrigerate the Caprese Quinoa Salad for about 30 minutes to let the flavors meld.

Serve:
- Serve the Caprese Quinoa Salad at room temperature or chilled.

Enjoy:
- Enjoy your refreshing and nutritious Caprese Quinoa Salad!

Feel free to customize the salad by adding extras like pine nuts, olives, or avocado if you like. This recipe is a great way to enjoy the classic Caprese flavors in a wholesome and satisfying salad.

www.ingramcontent.com/pod-product-compliance
Lightning Source LLC
LaVergne TN
LVHW081607060526
838201LV00054B/2122